Blogging for Business: A How-To Guide

ISBN: 1-4564-4008-X
ISBN-13: 9781456440084

Blogging for Business: A How-To Guide

A how-to guide for everything you need to succeed
In blogging for business.

Kristi Hines

VERTICAL MEASURES

Editorial coordination by: Elise Redlin-Cook
Designed by: David Gould
Volume editor: David Gould

2011

Table of Contents

Introduction

Why Your Business Should Be Blogging

Businesses of all shapes and sizes throughout every industry are blogging today, and for good reason. Blogging has come a long way from simply being a shared journal between friends and family, much like social media platforms such as Facebook have evolved from simply an online hangout for college students.

Any business, whether it is a local deli to a worldwide corporation can benefit from blogging in a variety of ways.

Blogging for Credibility

In the past, if you wanted to be considered an expert in something, you would have to become a published author. Now, in the digital age, a blogger can achieve a similar position within their niche or industry by creating quality content on a specific topic and developing an engaged community around that content.

Blogging for Reputation Management

With the rise of review sites that carry a strong weight with search engines, it is easy for a business to find one or more negative items in the search results for their company or brand name. Creating strong blogs can help a business rank good content about themselves above the less than desirable reports.

Blogging for Search Engines

Even if you do not have any damaging content about your business on the web, you would still want the benefits of having great blog content to draw in search engines. Blog posts with keyword-rich titles can help you rank for very specific terms potential customers may be looking for, bringing them right to your website.

Blogging for Your Customers

Speaking of customers, a blog can be a great way to share information with them as well. You can use your blog to communicate with your customers about any of the following:

- Company updates—things about your company that your customers would like or be impressed by, including charity work or donations, in-depth team bios, major milestones such as years in business, etc.

- Product references—consider your blog as an extended, always-updating product or service manual with detailed how-to guides and ways to exceed expectations with what you have to offer.

Blogging for Your Industry

Thinking back to blogging for authority and credibility—especially if your business is B2B—blogging about the latest news in your industry can position your business as a leader in that industry. This may garner word of mouth references from your audience and even your competitors, who may enlist your services to help them with theirs.

Blogging for Lead Generation

The amount of leads that can be generated from a great blog post is amazing! If you can convince people why something would be good for them through a blog post and give a strong, non-sales pitch-like call to action, you are likely to gain their trust through the honesty of the content. In turn, they will be interested in ways that you can help them achieve what you have written about.

These are only just a few of the many reasons and benefits of blogging. Once you have determined what your goal is for business blogging, you are ready to get started.

Researching the Competition
The Foundation to Building Your Strategy

One of the beauties of business blogging is that, with some competitor research, you can learn what really works and what does not within your industry to accomplish your specific goals. There are many ways to find blogs by other bloggers or businesses that cover your niche or industry, from local businesses to worldwide entities. Here are a few methods to use.

Your Competitors

Most businesses are able to readily name two to three competitors in their industry. These are going to be your best starting points. Start by visiting your competitors' websites to see if they have their own blog.

Google Search

Of course, the next fastest way to find anything is via Google. Get started with searching for competitor blogs using the following search query formats:

- For blogs in a particular industry: industry blog, i.e. chiropractor blog, chiropractic blogs

- For local blogs in a particular industry: location industry blog, ie. new york deli blog

- For blogs by a particular company: company blog, i.e. Southwest blog

- For blogs by a particular person: "name" blog, i.e. "Bill Gates" blog

Blog Directories

Your next stop in competitor research is the land of blog directories. There are several great directories to choose from, including the following:

- Eaton Web—this directory includes the best blogs, listing them in order of importance based on a variety of popularity metrics. Categories including health, money, technology, education, real estate, and more are broken into several subcategories so you can easily find the top blogs in particular topics.

- Technorati—this directory has a broader list of categories (with technology only broken into "Info Tech" and "Gadgets"), but also has a powerful search engine to use for blogs and posts on certain topics. Blogs are listed by Technorati Authority, a rating based on the blog's incoming links during a short period of time from other blogs, determining its popularity.

Engaging Blogs

If you are specifically looking for blogs that do well with readers, then PostRank is the site for you. The topic breakdowns are not as comprehensive as the Eaton Web directory, but what you will find on this site are the top blogs based on audience engagement through blog comments and social sharing. So if you are looking to emulate blogs that build authority, bring in strong traffic, and help build community through reader participation and interaction, then PostRank will show you the right blogs to follow.

The easiest way to use the site is by searching for a specific topic. If available, they will suggest subtopics at the top of the search results as well as related topics in the right hand sidebar.

I've Found Competitors—Now What?

Now that you've found a few good competitors' blogs, the next thing to do is a little analysis. Based on your goals, what are these blogs doing right to achieve those goals? Do they have high blog comment volume? Do they have lead capture forms? Take notes about things you like and dislike about your competitors' blogs in terms of topics covered, design elements, etc. and use these notes to create the perfect blog for your industry.

Creating a Home
What Should Your Blog's Domain Be

The first thing that you must consider when it comes to creating a blog for your business is where it will reside. There are several options to choose from, as well as specific reasons for each.

On Your Company Domain

Your first option is to create your blog on your business' main domain, e.g. yourdomain.com. You can choose to place your blog on your main domain as a subdirectory, such as yourdomain.com/blog. The advantage to this approach is that your blog will be on your main website, which will make it easy for readers to switch from your blog straight to your business' website. Also, any links built to your blog or blog posts will help in increasing your main website's overall reputation in the eyes of search engines. Likewise, the blog will be able to pull from the main website's authority as well, which may help your articles get higher rankings.

Your other option on the company domain would be to create your blog on a subdomain, such as blog.yourdomain.com. Subdomains do not receive the authority of the root domain like a subdirectory does. Likewise, any links built to your blog would only help to increase the subdomain's authority, and not help the root domain.

If you are interested in the search value aspect, SEO expert Rand Fishkin[1] and Google's Matt Cutts[2] both recommend subdirectories over subdomains for blogs.

On a New Domain

Another option is to create your blog on a completely new domain. The reasoning behind this approach is to create a blog that is purely focused on the blog itself, and less on the company, even if the new domain inherits elements of design from the main company website. This approach is also used as a lead generation tactic: a company can create a blog which becomes a hub for a particular topic while not giving any kind of "corporate" feel.

On a Blog Publishing Service Domain

Services such as WordPress, Blogger, and TypePad allow you to create blogs on their website, with a URL of yourchoice.wordpress.com, yourchoice.blogspot.com, or yourchoice.typepad.com respectively.

The advantage to going with this approach is that you do not have to get involved with installing and managing a content management system on your own domain. You can simply create a blog and maintain it through the blog publishing services. If you are looking at blogging for reputation management, you can create multiple blogs on these services. Since they are on different domains, they may each begin to rank well for your company name, thus pushing any negative search results further down in the search results page. Each blog, of course, would need to be regularly updated with great content, and each would need to be linked to and promoted individually in order to gain and sustain their rankings.

The disadvantage to this approach is that you do not have as much control over your blog, from choosing and customizing designs to even possibly losing your content. While WordPress, Blogger, and TypePad have been going strong and do not show signs of slowing down any time in the near future, other blog publishing services have come and gone. The most recent example was Vox[3], whose service warned users that they were closing their doors in thirty days, and if they did not backup or transfer their content within that timeframe, it would be lost.

Now, let's take a look at the various blog platforms for self-hosted domains and hosted services in detail.

Comparing Platforms
Pros and Cons of Different Content Management Systems

Self-Hosted Blogging Platforms

If you decide to have your blog on your own domain, a subdomain, or a brand new domain, your next step is which blogging platform to choose from. The following are currently the most popular options for self-hosted platforms.

A look at the traffic trends shown above for these sites can help you understand the popularity of each blogging platform. While WordPress maybe be dropping a bit in traffic, they have stayed consistent as the top self-hosted blogging software in the last year, with over one million visits to their site each month for software downloads, themes, plugins, and support within the community driven forums.

Each of these platforms have their own pros and cons, as well as features which help different types of users. Let's look at some of the platforms in detail.

WordPress

http://www.wordpress.org/

WordPress is the top self-hosted blogging platforms with over 25 million users, and for good reason: it is a very end-user-friendly platform, good for those who are not necessarily designers or developers. As a full-time blogger, it is my platform of choice, and also the one I will refer to throughout the rest of this book.

The software itself is open source and free to download. Many hosting companies such as HostGator and GoDaddy offer free installation of WordPress through their hosting control panel.

There are thousands upon thousands of free themes, as well as more advanced premium themes to choose from to get the right look, feel, and functionality for your blog. For what WordPress and the theme cannot do, there are plugins that you can download that will probably get the job done. Between the themes and plugins, WordPress can be the most user-, search-, and visitor-friendly blogging platform available.

And how search-friendly is WordPress? Even Matt Cutts, the face of Google, uses WordPress for his own blog!

Drupal

http://www.drupal.org/

Drupal is a very developer-friendly platform that is used primarily as a content management system, which can also be used for blogs. The biggest complaint about the Drupal platform is that it doesn't have the same great look and feel as a WordPress site would. Drupal should only be used by those that are extremely proficient with coding.

Joomla

http://www.joomla.org/

Joomla is a blogging platform geared toward those who are more design-oriented, although developers and administrators enjoy it too. It isn't as user-friendly as WordPress yet, but it is increasing in popularity.

Movable Type

http://www.movabletype.com/

Movable Type is a platform that is not as well known overall, but used by major corporations like the ones shown above on the website. They boast one of the most advanced platforms in creating beautiful blogs and websites. It is free for developers and individual bloggers, but for multi-author blogs and businesses, the pricing starts at $395USD for 5 authors, $995 for 20 authors, and unlisted enterprise pricing plans.

Hosted Blogging Platforms

If you are looking for a blog that you can create quickly without having a domain of your own, the following are the most popular hosted blogging platforms.

The above graphs show the popularity of each network, which can be an indicator of the number of readers who visit blogs on these networks as a whole.

Blogger

http://www.blogspot.com/

Blogger, Google's own free hosted blog platform, allows you to create blogs quickly and easily. Although the templates on their site are not the greatest, you can find free Blogger themes template sites.

Blogger is supported by many widgets and plugins—not as many as self-hosted WordPress installations, but certainly more than most free hosted platforms. You can also modify the coding of the theme for minor additional changes in looks and functionality, including adding in SEO elements such as a meta description and title tag for all of your posts, which we will discuss later in the SEO section of this book.

WordPress.com

http://www.wordpress.com/

WordPress offers a free, hosted blogging solution in addition to their self-hosted software. The theme selection for WordPress.com is limited, with fewer than 100 themes to choose from and custom CSS coding only available to those who pay for premium upgrades. Plugins that are available for self-hosted WordPress users are not available to those using free or premium hosted accounts.

Otherwise, it is very user-friendly and quick to setup. WordPress is, however, on the lookout for sites that seem spammy—only promoting affiliate products, created for search engines and not visitors—and will deactivate them if they break any terms of service agreements.

TypePad

http://www.typepad.com/

TypePad is a premium hosted blogging service that offers built in SEO and social sharing functionality, as well as support. Starting at $8.95 a month, you can have one blog using their URL (yourblog.typepad.com) or re-directed to your own domain, and for $14.95 a month, you can have an unlimited number of blogs and a fully customizable design. Businesses can go to the $29.95 a month plan which features all of the above plus priority support.

Finding Your Bloggers
Who Will Be the Voice of Your Blog

The next big question is: who will be your business' bloggers? Depending on the size of your organization and the time each member currently has available for new tasks, finding bloggers could be simple or a challenge. Let's look at your options.

Looking Internally

Choosing people from inside your business is usually the smartest move because who knows your business better than those who are involved with running it on a day to day basis? If you have employees that are passionate about your business and your industry, then they likely will have a lot to say when it comes to writing about it. If you have passionate employees who also happen to be bloggers, then you are doubly lucky, as they would be the perfect choice for your business blog!

Having people from your own company do the blogging will help build them up as industry experts, which could come in quite handy when it comes to generating leads. People might specifically want to use your product or get on board with your services based on the fact that they know you have an educated, experienced team.

Outsourcing

Outsourcing your blog content can mean anything from getting a content development company to create your post, or simply looking for freelance writers to write about your industry.

If you go this route, you will want to make sure that whoever you choose knows your company's philosophy and what you are about. Feel free to give them topic ideas and the dates you would like to have the content returned by or, if you give them author access to your blogging platform, when you would like the posts to be entered by.

Guest Bloggers

Another way to supplement the content on your blog is by inviting guest bloggers to write for your site. You can offer to pay your guest bloggers like freelancers, but many will be happy to write for a blog in exchange for a link back to their site.

Finding Your Voice

Last, but not least, you will probably want to set a certain tone, or voice, for your blog. If you're not sure where to start on that, your best bet is to look at some of those blogs you found in your competitor research and decide which one you like the sound of best.

Do they speak very casually to their reader or formally? Do they share easy-to-digest content or very technical, advanced content? Which one do you like the best, and which one do you like the least. Which one do you think speaks the language of your desired audience the best?

When you start out with new writers, whether they are internal, outsourced, or guest bloggers, be sure to give them some samples so they can know what kind of post to write for you. That way you can get the perfect content the first time around.

Staying on Track
Creating Your Editorial Calendar

One of the most important things you will need to create for your business blog is an editorial calendar. It's easy when you are in the midst of working on paying client work to slack off on the internal, non-revenue projects such as your blog, but in order to have a successful blog, you must maintain it regularly.

The easiest way to maintain your blog calendar is through a program like Microsoft Office or online apps like the Google Calendar. This way, all of the blog writers can easily be added to the calendar. Alternatively, you can simply print out a calendar for all of your in-house employees (or email one in PDF format for remote employees or freelance writers to reference).

The things you will most want to keep track of are:

- Who is writing what posts, and when.

- When guest posts are going to be scheduled.

- What topics are to be covered (such as specific topics on a regular day of the week or a weekly theme topic).

- Regular series posts.

- Maintenance activities (such as who is in charge of moderating and responding to comments during the week).

- Special events (such as contests, discounts, and specials that need to be promoted during a certain time frame.

Choosing the Best Topics
What is Popular in Your Industry

Whether you're a business blogger, article marketer, copywriter, novelist, poet, student writing an essay, or any other form of writer, social networks can be a great research tool to finding what is hot now in your niche or industry. Social media can also be one of the best ways to beat a case of old-fashioned writer's block if you know where to look and setup some channels to be ready at your fingertips when you need it.

Here are some excellent ways to use social media to find what's popular in your industry.

Twitter for Monitoring Discussions

I personally like my inspiration in short, 140-character bites as it provides the spark to think about a topic. If you use a Twitter management tool such as Hoot-Suite, Tweetdeck, or CoTweet, you can easily monitor conversations on any given topic by simply setting up searches for particular keywords.

My personal tool of choice is HootSuite, because you can have many tabs, each with 10 columns of searches. You can use the keyword searches to simply see what is being talked about with regard to that topic, or go further with advanced Twitter search queries such as:

- **Keyword filter:links** for people discussing a topic with a link in their tweet so you can see a news item, article, or blog post on the topic. **-filter:links** removes the link so you can see people just talking about something.

- **Keyword ?** for people discussing a topic and asking a question—this can be a great way to generate writing ideas because you know people will be interested in your writing if you answer most asked questions.

- **Keyword :)** for people discussing a topic that they like, or **Keyword :(** for topics that they dislike—great way to come up with a top 10 list of things people like or hate about a certain subject.

Twitter for Monitoring Industry Leaders

Another way to be inspired is to simply see what leaders and authorities in a certain niche are talking about. But first, a good question is how to find industry experts.

- If you're looking for experts who blog, check out the Technorati search—just switch the slide over to blogs and search for a keyword. The results will bring you the highest authority blogs that are related to that topic.

- Twellow directory allows you to search by keywords that are found in Twitter profiles. The results are sorted by the people with the most followers, which is usually (though not always) a sign of an expert in that niche.

- Wefollow allows you to search Twitter users by particular keywords, and you can look at the people that have the most followers or the ones that are the most influential. Surprisingly, you'll find that the results vary between the two lists.

- Listorious lets you search among Twitter lists for particular topics. Check out the top 140 lists, which show the most followed of a collection of industry experts.

Once you have found leaders in your area, create or follow an already created Twitter list of the top writers in your niche and keep an eye on the things they talk about. Sometimes, you may find that you have a little extra to add to what they say, or maybe you disagree and have a better alternative to something they write about. This is a perfect thing to write about in your own blog or article networks like HubPages or Squidoo. Be sure that you mention the person who gave you the idea.

Another way to combine the world of experts with the above mentioned keyword or question searches is to setup a search of questions being asked of industry experts. You would be amazed by the writing topics that can be inspired by simply setting up a search for **@expert ? -filter:links**. Considering that some people have thousands to millions of followers, imagine how many questions are just waiting to be answered.

#3: Use LinkedIn Answers

Speaking of questions, another great place to find out what kind of questions are being asked in your niche or industry is within the LinkedIn Answers section. Once you sign into your LinkedIn account, simply use the search bar at the top right, select Answers from the dropdown menu, and enter your keyword.

If just reading questions doesn't inspire you, why not try answering some. Use the advanced search option to find keywords specifically in questions only, and check the option to look for only open questions.

I have found that when answering questions, on LinkedIn, Yahoo Answers, and even within blog comments, I have been inspired for a new article idea.

Facebook for Monitoring Discussions

Would you like to monitor topics being discussed on Facebook the same way you do on Twitter? There's a site for that also, although it's not as advanced as the Twitter search queries (which means no filtering out links or finding only questions). Kurrently lets you monitor up-to-the-minute status updates made from public Facebook profiles.

Although you can't do a search for questions only, you can include question phrases in your search, such as "how do I keyword". But even if you put the words in quotes, it will pull any status update with those words anywhere throughout it.

Niche Networks

If your niche or business is very specific and has networks that are focused specifically on that area, check out the network that caters to that specific audience. Some ideas on niche networks include:

- Active Rain for Real Estate professionals.

- Dogster for dog owners.

- Ballroom Dance Channel for dancers.

- Tennisopolis for tennis fans and players.

To find more niche specific networks, just Google your keyword and "social networks" or visit websites where you can create your own network (such as Ning) and search for networks built with their platform.

Inspiration for Writing on Popular Topics

What if you're not necessarily looking for just any topic to write about, but the topics that are going to be the most well-received by your target audience? The best way is to simply look at what's popular and trending right now. Here are some ways to find some great topics that are more likely to spread through the social media world and go viral.

Social Bookmarking Networks

If your aim is to get a lot of votes on Digg, or similar social bookmarking networks, why not check out what has recently and historically gained a lot of votes in your niche. The Digg search box allows you to look up any topic, then sort it by the Best Match, Most Dugg, or Newest results.

You can also use the sidebar to get results only from a certain time period (today through the last 30 days), narrow it down to items that have received 50+ to 5,000+ diggs, and sort by a particular media format. In the case of article writing, you'll want to go for news. You can also use advanced search queries such as: *-keyword* to remove unwanted related items from your keyword search.

If Digg doesn't cater to your industry, look at social bookmarking or voting networks that are more niche-specific such as:

- Sphinn for SEO to social media themes.

- Tip'd for financial news.

- Design Bump for design and freelance articles.

- Dzone for developers posts.

- BizSugar for small business topics.

Most Popular on Twitter

If your goal is to have the most tweets, then you'll want to check out the following sites to learn more about topics that get retweeted the most.

TweetMeme

Tweetmeme lets you see what topics are tweeted about the most in a variety of channels, such as comedy, entertainment, business, technology, sports, and more. You can view the items most retweeted today through the last seven days and sort the items by news, images, and videos.

You can also do a keyword search and sort by the most amount of tweets, age of the tweets (from the last day, week, or over a week old), search within categories, and filter items with 100+ or 1,000+ tweets.

Topsy

Topsy is a search engine powered by tweets that you search by simply entering any keyword. Like the Google search box, it will also suggest specific ideas or phrases for you to get started, or you can just enter a more basic keyword. You can search within the last hour, day, week, month, or all recorded tweets for a given keyword, and see the number of times those items have been retweeted.

Although you can't sort by the items with the number of retweets, what I find particularly useful on this network is the piece of information you can find when you click on the number of times the item has been retweeted.

You can also either see all of the retweets for a particular item, or you can see just the retweets by influential users.

This little piece of information helps you get to know not only what is popular throughout the mainstream Twitter community, but what topics are likely to get retweeted by the bigger players on Twitter. Hovering over a user's name, as shown above, shows the user's stats as well.

Most Popular on Facebook

It's Trending is a great site to find out what's being shared the most on Facebook. Although it doesn't have a search feature for particular topics, if your niche falls under Sports, Tech, Gaming, Entertainment, or Comedy, you can see the most shared items on Facebook in those areas.

You can also see what is most popular on a particular featured site, so if your writing subject is social media, you can see what topics by Mashable have been the most popular on Facebook.

Most Popular on Authority Blogs

PostRank is home to a directory of the most socially engaging blogs in al-most any niche or industry. You can search for your blog's topic to see what blogs are currently covering the same themes, and then see which posts on that blog get the most social shares, comments, and so on. To narrow the results, you can filter the post listing for Great or Best Posts to receive the top content by particular blog.

By hovering over the score, you can quickly see how that particular post was shared the most (e.g.Twitter, Delicious, Facebook, MySpace). This can help you de-cide what headlines and topics will be the most popular for your audience as well.

Writing Great Posts
A Step by Step Guide

There are certain elements of a blog post that need to be given special care in order for a post to be successful. Let's take a look at these elements and what you need to do to make sure they are optimized.

1. The Title / Headline

A great title for your post is essential for driving traffic to it, from social media to search engines. Take Twitter, for example. The first impression of your post will be the 140 character status update including just the title of your post. For search engines, it's the same: the title will be the first thing potential visitors read in the results.

When it comes to great titles, you should consider:

- Including the post's main keyword for search engines and social searches.

- Including a number. People like posts where they know what they are getting. So instead of "Tips to Keep Your Car in Tip Top Shape" you should do "10 Tips to Keep You Car in Tip Top Shape."

- Including a solution to a problem. If you know a common question in your industry, such as how to keep your pool chemical levels in check, then you should do a post entitled "10 Ways to Make Sure Chemicals in Your Pool Are at Safe Levels."

- Keep titles under 65 characters in length for search engine purposes. Anything after this point will be cut off with a "…".

2. Word Count

There is a lot of debate about the proper length of a blog post. Some say that you should keep it short and sweet with an average of 300-500 words per post. Others think that posts should be in-depth and complex, with a minimum of 1,000 words.

What you should be concerned about, more than the actual word count, is whether or not you are giving valuable information in each post. If you can deliver the content that you promise in the title of the post in a short post, then that is fine. If you can write a long post that isn't redundant and keeps your reader's interest, that is fine as well.

My rule of thumb is to never make the reader have to go elsewhere for information. You shouldn't do a post with 10 tips if the reader is going to have to leave your site to find out how to implement those 10 tips. You should either have enough content for each tip that the reader can implement them, or have a post that you can link to on your site that further explains how to do each item.

3. Breaking Up the Content

One of the biggest turn-offs when it comes to reading blog posts or articles is seeing big blocks of text, text, and nothing but text. You want your post to be easy to scan, so that if you get someone who wants to take a quick glance to see if they want to bookmark the post for later, they will see the gist of the article quickly and easily. This can be accomplished by:

- Using headers for major sections. Your post should contain headers using the <h2> or <h3> header tags in HTML, not only to easily divvy up the sections but also to be search engine friendly.

- Using images. Think about when you read books as a kid. You probably enjoyed the ones with lots of pictures over the ones that were solid text, right? Blog readers enjoy images similarly, especially if they are screenshots or photos that illustrate a point in the text.

- Using series posts. If you have an article that going to be excessively lengthy, consider taking the one post and breaking it into a series of posts. This will keep your readers coming back to your site for more.

- Using bullet points and numbered lists. Again, this helps break out individual items and make it easily scan-able.

- Using formatted text. Be sure to emphasize important phrases or statements in your post by using **bolded** and *italicized* text within the content.

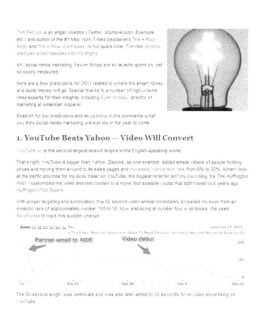

Mashable does a great job of breaking up their content using images and headers, as shown in this post above. It makes a post that has a lot of content easily scan-able for those looking for a particular topic and digestible for those who just want an idea of the overall goal of the post.

4. Call to Action

No matter what your post is about, or what industry you are in, you can have a call to action in each and every blog post. Calls to action can be anything from suggesting that the blog reader contact your business for help with any of the items recommended in the blog post to simply asking your readers for their opinion about the content of the post.

Asking readers for comments is an important way to build your blog's social proof. This means that whenever a new visitor comes to your blog, they will see that your posts have a lot of active discussion, telling the new visitor that your content is valuable and worth discussion.

Search Optimizing Your Blog
Bringing in Search Traffic

Now that you know what elements of a blog post are essential for your readers, let's look at what parts of the post (and the blog as a whole) are important to search engines so that more people can find your blog and, ultimately, your business.

There are tons and tons of search engine optimization tips that can be applied to websites, but here we are going to focus on the most important ones for your blog. The best part about blogs when it comes to search is that Google loves them, particularly the fact that blogs deliver fresh new content regularly and Google is quite fond of indexing new content. Blogs give search engine crawlers a reason to come back to your site often to find out if anything new is happening.

SEO for Your Blog

Matt Cutts, in a presentation at a WordPress seminar in 2009[4], said that "WordPress takes care of 80-90% of the mechanics of Search Engine Optimization."

How does WordPress do this? The WordPress platform (self-hosted) allows blog owners to incorporate plugins and themes which are optimized for search. For example, you can download and install the Platinum SEO Pack or All-in-One SEO Pack plugins for free to any WordPress theme. These plugins add extra options to the WordPress administrator dashboard for important SEO information.

Platinum SEO Plugin Options

This is version 1.2.8 | FAQ | Feedback | What is new in version 1.2.8? | Wordpress SEO options | Please Donate |

Pls. write a review or choose to link back, if you cannot donate

Click on option titles to get help!

Automatically do 301 redirects for permalink changes:	☑
Home Title:	All About Mal-Shis	Malshi	Malti Tzu	Shih-Tese
Home Description:	All About Mal-Shis is about the hybrid / designer dog mix between a Maltese and Shih Tzu, also known as Malti Tzu or Shih-Tese. Mal-
Home Keywords (comma separated):	mal-shi, mal-shis, malshi, malti tzu, shih-tese, shihtese, designer dog, hybrid dog, maltese, shih tzu
Canonical URLs:	☑
Rewrite Titles:	☑

Most of the fields are set for a default level of optimization. The ones you will want to make sure to fill in are the:

- Home Title—A 65-character title for your blog. Be sure to include your primary keywords here.

- Home Description—A 255-character description for your blog. Again, be sure to include your primary keywords. There is debate that the meta description doesn't count for much, but as long as Google and other search engines use your description in their search results, you should continue to use it as well, tailoring it to make searchers want to come to your site.

- Home Keywords—Meta keywords supposedly have little to no SEO value, but again, it doesn't hurt to enter them for the smaller search engines that still do use the information. Just be sure to keep the character count under 268 characters.

Permalinks

Another essential element for making your blog friendly for search are permalinks. These are what automatically set the links for new pages and posts on your site. For example, the default permalink for blog posts in WordPress is *http://yourblog.com/?p=123*. This has little to no SEO value.

What you will want to do is make sure your permalinks are creating URLs that incorporate the title of your post into the link, such as *http://yourblog.com/automotive-accessories-for-2011/*, which will help get your keywords emphasized in your title, meta description, and URL.

In WordPress, you can create better permalinks by going to your **Settings** > **Permalinks** and using the Custom Structure, as shown below.

If you are using a platform other than WordPress, be sure to lookup the platform's help documents to see if you can specify a permalink structure, unless the platform (like Blogger) automatically uses a good permalink structure to include your post's title in the URL.

Sitemaps

Another thing WordPress makes simple is the sitemap for your blog. Google XML Sitemaps plugin allow the blog owner to create a sitemap initially for the blog and submit it to Google Webmaster Tools as well as the webmaster centrals for Bing, Yahoo, and Ask. Not only does the plugin create the initial sitemap, but it will continue to keep the sitemap up to date when you add new content to the blog, continuing to ping each search engine immediately when you create new posts or pages.

SEO for Your Blog Posts

Along with the SEO options for your main blog, the two above mentioned plugins also offer SEO options for each of your posts. Again, the most important items are the title, description, and keywords.

These fields are not only valuable for search engines. Whenever someone goes to bookmark or share your blog post on social networks, many will automatically grab the title as anchor text for the link to your post and the description as a short summary of the post to go with it. Therefore, what you use in these fields could attract more visitors from social networking and bookmarking sites as well.

Alternatively, SEO plugins give you the option to not include a particular post in search engine listings. I have rarely used any of those options as I prefer everything to be indexed, giving my blog more overall strength, but in the case that you do have posts that you do not want indexed, the options below the keywords are the ones to go for.

Promoting Your Posts
Getting the Word Out

Now that you have written an amazing blog post, you will want to make sure that other's find it. Let's look at some ways to expose your blog post to your audience and beyond.

Social Networks

The first and most important place to publicize your latest blog post is with your connections on social networks. Here are the top social networks and how to use them to promote your blog posts.

Twitter

Twitter is one of the easiest networks to build followers, as well as one of the quickest to update with simple 140-character messages.

First, you will want to create a shortened URL for your blog post—you can use services like Bit.ly to shorten the URL as well as track statistics such as the number of retweets and clicks on the link to your post. You can also customize the Bit.ly URL with keywords, such as http://bit.ly/bloggingresources.

Once you have shortened your URL, you can promote blog posts on Twitter in the following ways.

1.   Tweet your new posts at three times during the day. In order to not repeat the exact same tweet, try to think of three different titles that could work for your post (such as "Great Blogging Resources", "15 Valuable Resources for Blogging", and "Great Resources for Bloggers") and tweet these variations with your shortened URL.

2.   Monitor conversation. Do Twitter searches for people who may be asking a question that your blog post can answer, such as creating a search for *"best blogging resource ?"* and answering it with your post.

3.   Send your latest post as a Direct Message. Services like Social Oomph allow you to set a 140 character greeting to your new followers auto-

matically. If you think your blog post is something that your followers would enjoy, use it as part of your welcome greeting. Just be sure to remind yourself to change that greeting whenever you have a new amazing blog post you want to share with everyone.

The following is a look at the inside of my own HootSuite, on a tab that is tracking my latest guest post.

Here you can see my Pending Tweets, which is where I schedule the three times a day to tweet my latest post. I also have a column tracking any retweets of that customized URL and one that is monitoring discussions from people asking for SEO help where I might be able to send my post as an answer to their question.

You can also see above the streams are a huge list of tabs. This will allow you to setup whole tabs based on specific posts you want to always promote, as well as tabs to monitor mentions of your Twitter username, your favorite Twitter list, and much more.

Facebook

Facebook is the top social network, and definitely a good place to promote blog posts. While you can use HootSuite to connect to your Facebook profile and send out a 140-character status update similar to the one sent to Twitter, I would suggest taking some extra time to do the following updates instead.

1. Post a link to your latest blog post on your personal profile and/or fan page wall. By doing your updates this way, your blog post will take up more eye-catching real estate, leading to more attention and clicks. You can include a thumbnail from your article, edit the title and description, as well as add your own comment.

2. For extra value and greater exposure, be sure to tag people, products, or brands that you mention in your blog post. You will have to become friends with them first, or you will have to like their page. This will possibly get your blog post added to their wall as well, which is viewable by their friends and fans. So in essence, even if you only have 10 friends, you could tag your post and have it appear on a fan page which has thousands of fans!

3. Find groups that would be interested in your post, join them, and then post your link on their wall (if allowed). If the group doesn't allow this, then you might have to settle for a simple status update of just text and the link.

4. Find fan pages where the fans would be interested in your post, like the page, and then post the page's wall, assuming that the wall default display shows posts by the page and others.

Please note that you shouldn't go spamming everyone's wall with blog posts—choose only the ones that you know will be a great value to the groups and fan pages that you add them to, such as a guide to using a network on the fan page of that network and within groups that are all about the network. This will ensure that you are not eventually reported as a spammer.

Google Buzz

If you have a Gmail account, you can connect to Google Buzz and your contacts through a more robust, Twitter-like platform within your Gmail account. You can update your followers by attaching a link to your status update, as well as selecting any photos from your post, and sending a visually appealing update.

If you do not want to update your status manually, you can also connect your Google Buzz account to your Twitter, which will bring all of your Twitter updates to your Buzz followers as well. Keep in mind these updates can be muted by your followers, and that the only way to get through to your followers is by updating directly on Buzz and not through other connected networks.

LinkedIn

Finally, if you have a professional profile on LinkedIn, you can have HootSuite send a simple status update with your latest blog post to your connection's news feed. Or, you can use LinkedIn's status update field to attach a link with photos and an additional comment in order to have a more noticeable update which should garner more attention and clicks through to your post.

An added bonus to just appearing in your news feed, your latest status update will show on your main LinkedIn profile as well so that new connections can see your articles and learn more about your expertise.

Blog Commenting
Benefits of Commenting and How to Do It Right

Though there is a lot of debate about the value of blog commenting as a form of link building, it is still a very popular linking strategy. This chapter covers some basic things you will probably encounter while blog commenting, and how to make sure you get your comment approved more times than not.

Benefits of Blog Commenting Links

First off, let's look at the benefits of blog commenting. There are five primary reasons we build links for websites. Here is what you need to look for to accomplish these goals with blog commenting.

Traffic

If you are looking to increase traffic to your website, your best bet is to comment on blogs that receive a lot of traffic that are in your niche or industry, without concern to whether the links will pass search engine value (dofollow) or whether they will be ignored by search engines (nofollow).

To find popular blogs in your niche, you can check out the variety of blog directories previously mentioned, including Technorati, Alltop, and PostRank.

Search Engine Results Positioning

For boosting Search Engine Results Positioning (SERPs) for a particular keyword phrase, you will want to find relevant blogs using dofollow (as you would for PageRank boosting), plus you will want to be able to use keyword anchor text for your link. This means that the link to your website should be associated with your main keyword phrase, such as *web design blog*. This is a bit tricky in terms of getting passed moderation (more on that in a bit). But there are two ways to be sure you are safe with using keyword anchor text:

1. You find a blog post where others do it. If there are other people getting approved using keywords in their name field as anchor text or anchor text links in the body of the comment, then you probably can too.

2.   If you search for your keywords and "Your Name@Your Keywords" you will find blogs using KeywordLuv. You will just need to enter Your Name@Your Keywords in the name field to get your website linked to your preferred keywords and anchor text.

Blog Post or Article Promotion

If you are blog commenting to boost PageRank, search rankings, or traffic to particular blog posts, you can search for blogs enabled with CommentLuv. These blogs allow you to have a link to your main website as well as a link to a post below your comment.

Typically, you can do this by simply entering your blog URL or your author page/profile URL in the website field and CommentLuv will usually pull up your latest post (assuming your blog has a working RSS feed). If you want the option to pull up your latest 10 posts, you can create a free account on ComLuv and then have access to your latest posts, linked to by their titles.

You can also promote articles using CommentLuv that are on particular article directories including EzineArticles, HubPages, Squidoo, or any network that allows an RSS feed for articles by a particular author.

Spam Filters

There are several roadblocks that you can run into when blog commenting, especially when you are trying to get a link added to your comment. The biggest is going to be spam filters.

Akismet

Akismet is the top spam filter protection for WordPress blogs, both self-hosted domains and on the WordPress.com site. The challenge with Akismet is that it only takes a few bloggers to mark you as spam before you end up triggering one of the many criteria that their database checks for, and once you're in, you will have to request to be removed from their database. But of course, if you get marked as spam again, you'll be back in it again.

How do you know if you have been tagged as spam by Akismet? Typically, your comment will either be approved automatically or go into moderation. If you submit your comment, and it doesn't show it as being in moderation, then you might want to email the blog owner to let them know you just commented and it didn't show up on the site.

If you submit your comment on a blog post that is older than 30 days and get a white screen, then congratulations—you have found an Akismet protected blog that has turned on the option to delete any spam comments on older posts without it ever being recorded in the blogger's spam or moderation folder. Your comment, hence, will never be seen. Your only shot of getting a comment on that site at this stage will be to comment on a post that is less than 30 days old and email the blog owner to let them know you are in their spam filter.

Drupal

Drupal blogs (usually the ones you have to login or register for) also have a spam filtering system. You will know you have been caught by it because you will receive a warning when you submit your comment that it looks like spam because of the link in the body of the comment text. At this point, you'll be prompted to enter a CAPTCHA—after that, it could go live or be sent to moderation.

Alternatively, it may simply tell you it is not going to approve your comment at all. You can try changing your keyword phrase to less keywords or something different. And if this doesn't work, then your comment is probably not going to go through at all with any link in the comment body.

Standing Out From the Spammers

So if you do comment on a site that is heavily moderated or has a spam filter in place, how can you stand out and make yourself look like a legitimate commenter and not a spammer?

Gravatars

One of the most important ways to stand out from spammers in someone's spam filter is by the use of a Gravatar, which puts a photo next to your comment. As a blogger who uses Akismet, I can tell you that 99% of the spam never has a Gravatar, so if your comment does end up in the spam filter it will stand out much better if you have your picture next to it.

Profiles

If a site requires you to register to submit a comment, be sure to fill out some details in the profile. It only takes about an extra minute to fill out a few fields and maybe add an image if the profile asks for one, and it will make you look less like a spammer and more like a real person.

Spammers usually do one of two things: they do one comment on the highest PR post they can find on a site, or they hit as many posts as they can get their hands on. Your best bet is to do two comments on your first visit, on your target (most relevant or higher PR) post and on a recent post. If you want to continue to be able to comment at that blog, you will want to subscribe to comments (if that is an option) so if the blogger replies to you, you will be notified via email and can come back and answer. I have seen some bloggers that approve a comment and reply, and if the person doesn't come back, delete it shortly thereafter (or strip the link) assuming they were a spammer.

Moderation

The other major roadblock in blog commenting is moderation. Sometimes you think you have gotten lucky because you submitted your comment and it was approved automatically. But don't celebrate too soon. You might want to check back in a few days to make sure it is still there. Some sites will allow any comment to approve, but then will strip the link or delete it completely later on.

Getting Links in the Website Field of Your Comment Approved

On WordPress, Blogspot, or other websites that offer the standard name, email address, and website fields, your best chance of getting your comment approved is to follow commenting policy, stated or implied. If you find a comment policy, read it and don't break it, and your comment should get approved. If you don't see anything that explicitly says what their commenting policy allows or doesn't allow, take a look at previously approved comments. Is everyone using a real name or nickname? Then keywords probably aren't allowed in the name field, and if you try it, your comment will not get approved. Just follow the trend.

Getting Links in the Body of the Comment Approved

Probably the biggest spammer red flag are comments with a link embedded in the body of the comment. If the blog allows you to add a link in a website field, I would go with that first over adding the link to the body of the comment to get it approved. But if you don't have that as an option (as on Drupal blogs or others that you have to register for or connect with Twitter / Facebook) and you simply must have the link in the body of the comment, you have three options.

1. Include the link as your "signature" like you would in an email. Sometimes this will slip by moderation.

2. Include your link only if it answers a question from the blog post or another commenter. If the blog post says "where can I buy dog food at a good price?" and your link is a discount pet food supply store, then it might be welcome.

3. Include your link only if it somehow adds value to the post. If the blog post is about website analytics (preferably a comparison of services out there and not simply an advertisement post about one service), and your link is to an analytics service, you can include it as an additional resource for people to check out when comparing analytics programs. Listing some differences and benefits of your analytics program compared to the ones listed in the post would also be a plus.

4. If none of this works for you, find blogs that have approved comments with links in their comment text. Chances are, they will be spammy, but if others have spammed it, you probably can too. Just make sure the other links aren't really trashy and you should be in okay company.

In short, your link needs to add value to the post or discussion. Period. Or it's not getting approved unless you luck out on a site that has relaxed moderation.

A great post is not going to get you far and neither is a comment that has nothing to do with the post itself, no matter how long and intelligent it sounds. It is a time sucker, but you are going to have to read the post and make your comment a response to the post, or a response to another commenter's comment. Be a valuable commenter, not a comment spammer.

Generating Leads
Turning Readers into Customers

So how do you turn your regular blog readers into potential customers, besides having great calls to action in your blog posts? Getting your readers on an email list is definitely one of the best ways, due to the power of email marketing.

One thing that blog readers are used to seeing these days are opt-in forms asking for their name and address in exchange for some kind of free item, typically an e-book, whitepaper/report, or auto-responder course (people signup to receive a series of emails sent either daily or weekly for a certain period of time).

Free Content Creation

Creating all of these items can be quite simple if you already have content on your website, blog, or article sites. You can simply repurpose your content that you have used elsewhere as your free giveaway. The best way to do this is to take content that is older, update it, and then essentially repackage it. Some ideas include:

- Taking ten articles on ways to care for your car and turning it into an e-book or auto-responder course.

- Taking some technical findings or statistics that would be interesting to your audience and turning it into a whitepaper/report.

The simplest way to create an e-book or whitepaper (without buying more software and having to learn how to use it) is to create the document in Microsoft Word 2007+ and use the built in **Save As** > **PDF** converter.

Alternately, if you do not yet have a lot of content, you will need to write something (or hire someone to write some content for you) as your giveaway.

Opt-In Forms

Then, you will want to incorporate your current mailing list service opt-in form (such as Aweber, MailChimp, Salesforce, etc.) in your blog. The best places to place these forms are on your sidebar and/or at the end of blog posts.

There are also plugins that will allow you to have a popup opt-in form that comes up after readers have been on your site for specific times. These are increasing in popularity, but are typically reserved for the Internet marketing niche and not favored by many website visitors.

While they promise they will boost the number of subscribers to your email list, they will also increase the number of people who leave your site immediately because they are annoyed by them. Again, simply having your opt-in in your sidebar or at the end of posts should be ample enough exposure for the opt-in without being over intrusive.

Analyzing Your Success
Analytics for Your Blog

When it comes to finding out how successful your blog is, you will want to make sure to incorporate analytics programs into your blog platform. If you already use Google Analytics and your blog is on your main domain, then including your Google Analytics JavaScript code in your blog template/theme will ensure that the stats for your blog are tracked as well. If your blog is on another domain, then you will need to create a new domain your Google Analytics account to track it separately. This may only work for self-hosted blogs and blogs on platforms that support Analytics.

Here are some good ways to use Google Analytics to learn more about your blog's performance and ways to improve your content.

Goals

If your blog is on the same site as your main domain, you can easily setup goals (if you haven't already). Goals can be anything from a specified length of time you want visitors to be on your site to a URL to a thank you page that visitors receive after purchasing something from your site or signing up for your mailing list. Once you have setup your goals, you can easily see which keywords or referring sites leading to your blog are resulting in conversions.

Keyword	None	Visits	Request Info	Contact Us	Goal Conversion Rate
link building		424	0.94%	0.00%	0.94%
(content targeting)		150	8.00%	0.67%	8.67%
link building service		118	3.39%	0.85%	4.24%
what is link building		103	0.00%	0.00%	0.00%
social media marketing		60	3.33%	0.00%	3.33%

Referring Sites

It's obviously great to know where your traffic is coming from, but referring sites for your blog can also help you determine whether your promotion efforts are paying off with certain social networks and forums. If you notice you are putting the same amount of energy into several networks, but only a few of them are producing good results (like traffic and conversions) then you will know to refocus your efforts on the worthwhile networks and spend less time on ones that are not bringing better results to your blog.

Source	None	Visits	Request Info	Contact Us	Goal Conversion Rate
google.com		586	0.51%	0.00%	0.51%
twitter.com		273	0.73%	0.00%	0.73%
stumbleupon.com		187	0.00%	0.00%	0.00%
hootsuite.com		98	0.00%	0.00%	0.00%
facebook.com		92	0.00%	0.00%	1.09%

Site Search

Site Search is a great feature for determining what your blog visitors want when they use the search box on your site, as well as what pages they are searching for. So if you see that people are performing a lot of searches on your homepage for the keyword "Twitter," maybe it's a signal that you need to put a link to your company's Twitter on the homepage or a link to your Twitter articles there.

Top Site Searches	Searc...	% Searches	Top Searched Content	Searches	% Searches
thesis	9	3.28%		114	41.61%
stumbleupon	6	2.19%	/entrance	32	11.68%
hootsuite	5	1.82%	/category/blogging	8	2.92%
thesis customize menu	5	1.82%	/archives	7	2.55%
view full report			/guest-post-opportunities	6	2.19%
			view full report		

Checklist: Blogging for Reputation Management

Since reputation management requires a different approach compared to other reasons for blogging, I thought I would share a few items that you will need to make sure to do when it comes to blogging for reputation management.

- Create blogs on unique domains, as opposed to on your main website. Subdomains are also a good approach to creating new sites that will be listed individually by Google once ranked.

- Take advantage of free blogging networks including Blogspot, WordPress, Posterous, Tumblr, Livejournal, and Xanga. Create a subdomain name based on the reputation that needs to be reclaimed, ie. the company name, brand name, or person's name. This will give you a URL of *name*.wordpress.com or similar.

- Think of a unique topic, if possible, for each blog. For example, if the business needing the reputation boost sells pool supplies, you could create blogs on pool safety, pool accessories, pool party planning, pool design, etc.

- Be sure the title of the blog is or includes the company name, brand name, or person's name. For example, *Name*'s Guide to _____.

- If available, create a username that matches the reputation that needs to be reclaimed that will be listed as the author of the posts.

- When possible, use a link widget in the sidebar to link to other online entities of the company, brand, or person, including the other free blogs and social profiles.

- Maintaining content for so many sites may prove to be a challenge. Start with using content that you already have—if you have user manuals for a product; for example, make "how-to" posts that are based off of a page in the manual. Break larger pieces of content into bite sizes. Repurpose content from your main blog to the smaller blogs (such as taking a top 10 list and doing a post on each of the 10 items in the list).

- Consider freelance writers or content providers such as Vertical Measures for continuing to add unique content to each blog.

- Bookmark your blogs. Social bookmarks are easy links that you can build to each blog site. You can do them yourself to major networks, or use social bookmarking services such as Wyzo Marketing where you can get 300 social bookmarking backlinks for $9.90.

- Link to your blogs when possible, from your main site's blog and article marketing efforts. As with any site, the more links you build to the blogs, the higher they will move up in search rankings and will eventually outrank your negative search results.

Top Topics for Any Niche or Industry

Struggling to figure out new topics for your blog? Want to create a post that gets attention on a particular social network or community? Try out these topic ideas for your niche or industry! Change the number to fit however many you can find—top ten lists are popular!

- Top # Twitter Users in Your Niche / Industry (use Twellow and Wefollow to find them!)

- Top # Tweets in Your Niche / Industry (use Topsy and Tweetmeme to find them!)

- Top # Facebook Pages in Your Niche / Industry (Browse Facebook Pages to find them!)

- Top # Forums in Your Niche / Industry (search forum:*yourindustry* in Google to find them!)

- Top # Hashtags for Your Niche / Industry (use Hashtags to find them!)

- Top # Popular Videos in Your Niche / Industry (use YouTube and Vimeo to find them!)

- Top # Popular Stories in Your Niche / Industry (use Digg, StumbleUpon, and Topsy to find them!)

- Top # Rising Trends in Your Niche / Industry (use Google Insights to find them!)

- Top # Blogs in Your Niche / Industry (use Technorati, PostRank, and Eaton Blog Directory to find them!)

As you can see, there are many ways to create lists and top ten style posts using information that is already out there. These types of posts usually resonate well with readers and can lead to recognition by those that you list.

Also, don't consider them one-off posts. Topics like popular stories in your niche could be done periodically, such as Top # Popular Stories in Your Niche / Industry for May, 2010, and so on.

Resources

Want to learn more about blogging? Don't miss the following resources!

Sites Mentioned Throughout Book

Page 1

Eaton Web - http://portal.eatonweb.com/

Page 2

PostRank – http://www.postrank.com/
Technorati – http://technorati.com/

Page 6

Matt Cutt's Blog – http://www.mattcutts.com/blog/

Page 13

HootSuite – http://hootsuite.com

Page 14

Listorious – http://listorious.com/
Technorati search – http://technorati.com/
Twellow – http://www.twellow.com/
Wefollow – http://wefollow.com/

46

Page 15

Active Rain – http://activerain.com/
Ballroom Dance Channel – http://ballroomdancechannel.ning.com/
Dogster – http://www.dogster.com/
Kurrently – http://www.kurrently.com/
LinkedIn Answers – http://www.linkedin.com/answers/
Tennisopolis – http://tennisopolis.com/
Yahoo Answers – http://answers.yahoo.com/

Page 16

BizSugar – http://www.bizsugar.com/
Design Bump – http://designbump.com/
Digg – http://digg.com
Dzone – http://www.dzone.com
Sphinn – http://sphinn.com/
Tip'd – http://tipd.com/
Tweetmeme – http://tweetmeme.com/

Page 17

It's Trending – http://www.itstrending.com/
PostRank – http://www.postrank.com/
Topsy – http://topsy.com/

Page 25

GoogleWebmasterTools–https://www.google.com/webmasters/tools/home?hl=en

Page 27

Bit.ly – http://bit.ly/
Social Oomph – http://www.socialoomph.com/

Page 31

Alltop – http://alltop.com/
PostRank – http://www.postrank.com/

Technorati – http://technorati.com/

Page 32

Akismet – http://akismet.com/
KeywordLuv – http://www.scratch99.com/wordpress-plugin-keywordluv/
ComLuv – http://comluv.com/
CommentLuv – http://commentluv.com/

Page 33

Gravatar – http://gravatar.com/

Page 42

Vertical Measures – http://www.verticalmeasures.com/services/content-development/
Wyzo Marketing – http://www.wyzomarketing.com/social-bookmarking/

Page 43

Browse Facebook Pages – http://www.facebook.com/pages/browser.php
Digg – http://digg.com
Eaton Blog Directory – http://portal.eatonweb.com/
Google Insights – http://www.google.com/insights/search/
Hashtags – http://hashtags.org/
PostRank – http://www.postrank.com/
StumbleUpon – http://www.stumbleupon.com/
Technorati – http://technorati.com/
Topsy – http://topsy.com/
Tweetmeme – http://tweetmeme.com/
Twellow – http://www.twellow.com/
Vimeo – http://vimeo.com
Wefollow – http://wefollow.com/
YouTube – http://www.youtube.com/

References

1. Root Domains, Subdomains vs Subfolders and The Microsite Debate by Rand Fishkin on SEOMoz
2. Subdomains and Subdirectories by Matt Cutts
3. Six Apart Shuts Down Vox by Scott Gilbertson on Wired
4. SEO for Bloggers by Matt Cutts

The Vertical Measure How-To Guide Series Available Now

The Vertical Measures How-To Guide Series is for marketers, entrepreneur and executives that are ready to embrace emerging technologies that are taking businesses to the next level. The books highlight tactics that are worth focusing time and effort towards as well as those pointing out pitfalls to avoid.

The series provides deep insights into the world of emerging business technologies and covers topics including; Keyword Research, Facebook, Twitter, Local Search Marketing, Blogging and more.

- Succinct tactics for companies who are either using or plan to use new technologies to grow their business
- Written by industry experts with hands on experience in the field or discipline described
- Written specifically with the business and/or marketing user in mind –combining solid technical expertise with savvy advice.

www.ingramcontent.com/pod-product-compliance
Lightning Source LLC
Chambersburg PA
CBHW061036050326
40689CB00012B/2855